MW01502516

How I Wrote "The Raven"

Edgar Allan Poe

Fredonia Books
Amsterdam, The Netherlands

How I Wrote "The Raven"

by
Edgar Allan Poe

ISBN: 1-4101-0494-X

Fredonia Books
Amsterdam, The Netherlands
http://www.fredoniabooks.com

HOW I WROTE "THE RAVEN"

EDGAR ALLAN POE.

CHARLES DICKENS, in a note now lying before me, alluding to an examination I once made of the mechanism of *Barnaby Rudge*, says—"By the way, are you aware that Godwin wrote his *Caleb Williams* backwards? He first involved his hero in a web of difficulties, forming the second volume, and then, for the first, cast about him for some mode of accounting for what had been done."

I cannot think this the *precise* mode of procedure on the part of Godwin—and indeed what he himself acknowledges, is not altogether in accordance with Mr. Dickens' idea—but the author of *Caleb Williams* was too good an artist not to perceive the advantage derivable from at least a somewhat similar process. Nothing is more clear than that every plot, worth the name, must be elaborated to its *dénouement* before anything be attempted with the pen. It is only with the *dénouement* constantly in view that we can give a plot its indispensable air of consequence, or causation, by making the incidents, and especially the tone at all points, tend to the development of the intention.

There is a radical error, I think, in the usual mode of constructing a story.   Either history affords a thesis—or one is suggested by an incident of the day—or, at best, the author sets himself to work in the combination of striking events to form merely the basis of his narrative—designing, generally, to fill in with description, dialogue, or autorial comment, whatever crevices of fact, or action, may, from page to page, render themselves apparent.

I prefer commencing with the consideration of an *effect*. Keeping originality *always* in view—for he is false to himself who ventures to dispense with so obvious and so easily attainable a source of interest—I say to myself, in the first place, "Of the innumerable effects, or impressions, of which the heart, the intellect, or (more generally) the soul is susceptible, what one shall I, on the present occasion, select?" Having chosen a novel, first, and secondly a vivid effect, I consider whether it can be best wrought by incident or tone—whether by ordinary incidents and peculiar tone, or the converse, or by peculiarity both of incident and tone—afterward looking about me (or rather within) for such combinations of event or tone, as shall best aid me in the construction of the effect.

I have often thought how interesting a magazine paper might be written by any author who would—that is to say, who could —detail, step by step, the processes by which any one of his compositions attained its ultimate point of completion. Why such a paper has never been given to the world, I am much at a loss to say—but, perhaps, the autorial vanity has had more to do with the omission than any one other cause. Most writers— poets in especial—prefer having it understood that they compose by a species of fine frenzy —an ecstatic intuition—and would positively shudder at letting the public take a peep behind the scenes, at the elaborate and vacillating crudities of thought—at the true purposes seized only at the last moment—at the innumerable glimpses of idea that arrived not at the maturity of full view—at the fully matured fancies discarded in despair as unmanageable—at the cautious selections and rejections—at the painful erasures and interpolations—in a word, at the wheels and pinions— the tackle for scene-shifting—the step-ladders and demontraps—the cock's feathers, the red paint and the black patches which in ninety-nine cases out of the hundred constitute the properties of the literarv *histrio.*

I am aware, on the other hand, that the case is by no means common, in which an author is at all in condition to retrace the steps by which his conclusions have been attained. In general, suggestions, having arisen pell-mell, are pursued and forgotten in a similar manner.

For my own part, I have neither sympathy with the repugnance alluded to, nor, at any time, the least difficulty in recalling to mind the progressive steps of any of my compositions; and, since the interest of an analysis, or reconstruction, such as I have considered a *desideratum,* is quite independent of any real or fancied interest in the thing analyzed, it will not be regarded as a breach of decorum on my part to show the *modus operandi* by which some one of my own works was put together. I select "The Raven," as the most generally known. It is my design to render it manifest that no one point in its composition is referable either to accident or intuition—that the work proceeded, step by step, to its completion with the precision and rigid consequence of a mathematical problem.

Let us dismiss, as irrelevant to the poem, *per se*, the circumstance—or say the necessity —which, in the first place, gave rise to the intention of composing *a* poem that should suit at once the popular and the critical taste.

We commence, then, with this intention.

The initial consideration was that of extent. If any literary work is too long to be read at one sitting, we must be content to dispense with the immensely important effect derivable from unity of impression—for, if two sittings be required, the affairs of the world inter- fere, and everything like totality is at once destroyed. But since, *ceteris paribus*, no poet can afford to dispense with *anything* that may advance his design, it but remains to be seen whether there is, in extent, any advantage to counterbalance the loss of unity which attends it. Here I say no, at once. What we term a long poem is, in fact, merely a succession of brief ones—that is to say, of brief poetical effects. It is needless to demonstrate that a poem is such, only inasmuch as it intensely excites, by elevating, the soul; and all intense excitements are, through a psychal necessity, brief. For this reason, at least one-half of the *Paradise Lost* is essentially prose—a suc- cession of poetical excitements interspersed,

effect

totality — unity of effect

inevitably, with corresponding depressions—the whole being deprived, through the extremeness of its length, of the vastly important artistic element, totality, or unity, of effect.

It appears evident, then, that there is a distinct limit, as regards length, to all works of literary art—the limit of a single sitting—and that, although in certain classes of prose composition, such as *Robinson Crusoe,* (demanding no unity), this limit may be advantageously overpassed, it can never properly be overpassed in a poem. Within this limit, the extent of a poem may be made to bear mathematical relation to its merit—in other words, to the excitement or elevation—again in other words, to the degree of the true poetical effect which it is capable of inducing; for it is clear that the brevity must be in direct ratio of the intensity of the intended effect:—this, with one proviso—that a certain degree of duration is absolutely requisite for the production of any effect at all.

Holding in view these considerations, as well as that degree of excitement which I deemed not above the popular, while not below the critical taste, I reached at once what I conceived the proper *length* for my intended poem

—a length of about one hundred lines. It is, in fact, a hundred and eight.

My next thought concerned the choice of an impression, or effect, to be conveyed: and here I may as well observe that, throughout the construction, I kept steadily in view the design of rendering the work *universally* appreciable. I should be carried too far out of my immediate topic were I to demonstrate a point upon which I have repeatedly insisted, and which, with the poetical, stands not in the slightest need of demonstration—the point, I mean, that Beauty is the sole legitimate province of the poem. A few words, however, in elucidation of my real meaning, which some of my friends have evinced a disposition to misrepresent. That pleasure which is at once the most intense, the most elevating, and the most pure, is, I believe, found in the contemplation of the beautiful. When, indeed, men speak of Beauty, they mean, precisely, not a quality, as is supposed, but an effect—they refer, in short, just to that intense and pure elevation of *soul—not* of intellect, or of heart—upon which I have commented, and which is experienced in consequence of contemplating "the beautiful." Now I designate Beauty as the province of the poem, merely because

Beauty — an elevation of the soul

it is an obvious rule of Art that effects should be made to spring from direct causes—that objects should be attained through means best adapted for their attainment—no one as yet having been weak enough to deny that the peculiar elevation alluded to is *most readily* attained in the poem. Now the object, Truth, or the satisfaction of the intellect, and the object Passion, or the excitement of the heart, are, although attainable, to a certain extent, in poetry, far more readily attainable in prose. Truth, in fact, demands a precision, and Passion, a *homeliness* (the truly passionate will comprehend me) which are absolutely antagonistic to that Beauty which, I maintain, is the excitement, or pleasurable elevation, of the soul. It by no means follows from anything here said, that passion, or even truth, may not be introduced, and even profitably introduced, into a poem—for they may serve in elucidation, or aid the general effect, as do discords in music, by contrast—but the true artist will always contrive, first, to tone them into proper subservience to the predominant aim, and, secondly, to enveil them, as far as possible, in that Beauty which is the atmosphere and the essence of the poem.

Regarding, then, Beauty as my province,

my next question referred to the *tone* of its highest manifestation—and all experience has shown that this tone is one of *sadness*. Beauty of whatever kind, in its supreme development, invariably excites the sensitive soul to tears. Melancholy is thus the most legitimate of all the poetical tones.

The length, the province, and the tone, being thus determined, I betook myself to ordinary induction, with the view of obtaining some artistic piquancy which might serve me as a key-note in the construction of the poem— some pivot upon which the whole structure might turn. In carefully thinking over all the usual artistic effects—or more properly *points*, in the theatrical sense—I did not fail to perceive immediately that no one had been so universally employed as that of the *refrain*. The universality of its employment sufficed to assure me of its intrinsic value, and spared me the necessity of submitting it to analysis. I considered it, however, with regard to its susceptibility of improvement, and soon saw it to be in a primitive condition. As commonly used, the *refrain*, or burden, not only is limited to lyric verse, but depends for its impression upon the force of monotone—both in sound and thought. The pleasure is deduced solely from the sense of identity—of repetition. I resolved to diversify, and so vastly heighten, the effect, by adhering, in general, to the monotone of sound, while I continually varied that of thought: that is to say, I determined to produce continuously novel effects, by the variation *of the application* of the *refrain*—the *refrain* itself remaining, for the most part, unvaried.

These points being settled, I next bethought me of the *nature* of my *refrain*. Since its application was to be repeatedly varied, it was clear that the *refrain* itself must be brief, for there would have been an insurmountable difficulty in frequent variations of application in any sentence of length. In proportion to the brevity of the sentence, would, of course, be the facility of the variation. This led me at once to a single word as the best *refrain.*

The question now arose as to the *character* of the word. Having made up my mind to a *refrain*, the division of the poem into stanzas was, of course, a corollary: the *refrain* forming the close to each stanza. That such a close, to have force, must be sonorous and susceptible of protracted emphasis, admitted no doubt: and these considerations inevitably led me to the long *o* as the most sonorous vowel,

tone = melancholy (handwritten)

in connection with *r* as the most producible consonant.

The sound of the *refrain* being thus determined, it became necessary to select a word embodying this sound, and at the same time in the fullest possible keeping with that melancholy which I had predetermined as the tone of the poem. In such a search it would have been absolutely impossible to overlook the word "Nevermore." In fact, it was the very first which presented itself.

The next *desideratum* was a pretext for the continuous use of the one word "nevermore." In observing the difficulty which I at once found in inventing a sufficiently plausible reason for its continuous repetition, I did not fail to perceive that this difficulty arose solely from the preassumption that the word was to be so continuously or monotonously spoken by *a human* being—I did not fail to perceive, in short, that the difficulty lay in the reconciliation of this monotony with the exercise of reason on the part of the creature repeating the word. Here, then, immediately arose the idea of a *non*-reasoning creature capable of speech; and, very naturally, a parrot, in the first instance, suggested itself, but was superseded forthwith by a Raven, as equally capable

reconciliation of monotony of a reasonable creature (handwritten)

of speech, and infinitely more in keeping with the intended *tone*.

I had now gone so far as the conception of a *supremeness*, or perfection, at all points, I Raven—the bird of ill omen—monotonously repeating the one word, "Nevermore," at the conclusion of each stanza, in a poem of melancholy tone, and in length about one hundred lines. Now, never losing sight of the object asked myself—"Of all melancholy topics, what, according to the *universal* understanding of mankind, is the *most* melancholy?" Death— was the obvious reply. "And when," I said, "is this most melancholy of topics most poetical?" From what I have already explained at some length, the answer, here also, is obvious—"When it most closely allies itself to *Beauty:* the death, then, of a beautiful woman is, unquestionably, the most poetical topic in the world—and equally is it beyond doubt that the lips best suited for such topic are those of a bereaved lover."

I had now to combine the two ideas, of a lover lamenting his deceased mistress and a Raven continuously repeating the word "Nevermore"—I had to combine these, bearing in mind my design of varying, at every turn, the *application* of the word repeated; but the only intelligible mode of such combination is that of imagining the Raven employing the word in answer to the queries of the lover. And here it was that I saw at once the opportunity afforded for the effect on which I had been depending—that is to say, the effect of the *variation of application*. I saw that I could make the first query propounded by the lover—the first query to which the Raven should reply "Nevermore"—that I could make this first query a commonplace one—the second less so —the third still less, and so on—until at length the lover, startled from his original *nonchalance* by the melancholy character of the word itself—by its frequent repetition—and by a consideration of the ominous reputation of the fowl that uttered it—is at length excited to superstition, and wildly propounds queries of a far different character—queries whose solution he has passionately at heart—propounds them half in superstition and half in that species of despair which delights in self-torture—propounds them not altogether because he believes in the prophetic or demoniac character of the bird (which. reason assures him, is merely repeating a lesson learned by rote) but because he experiences a frenzied pleasure in so modeling his questions as to receive from the *expected* "Nevermore" the most delicious because the most intolerable of sorrow. Perceiving the opportunity thus afforded me—or, more strictly, thus forced upon me in the progress of the construction—I first established in mind the climax, or concluding query—that to which "Nevermore" should be in the last place an answer—that in reply to which this word "Nevermore" should involve the utmost conceivable amount of sorrow and despair.

Here then the poem may be said to have its beginning—at the end, where all works of art should begin—for it was here, at this point of my preconsiderations, that I first put pen to paper in the composition of the stanza.

> " 'Prophet,' said I, 'thing of evil! prophet still if bird or devil!
> By that heaven that bends above us—by that God we both adore,
> Tell this soul with sorrow laden, if within the distant Aidenn,
> It shall clasp a sainted maiden whom the angels name Lenore—
> Clasp a rare and radiant maiden whom the angels name Lenore.'
> Quoth the raven 'Nevermore.' "

I composed this stanza, at this point, first that, by establishing the climax, I might the

better vary and graduate, as regards seriousness and importance. the preceding queries of
the lover—and, secondly, that I might definite-
ly settle the rhythm, the meter. and the length
and general arrangement of the stanza—as
well as graduate the stanzas which were to
precede, so that none of them might surpass
this in rhythmical effect. Had I been able, in
the subsequent composition, to construct more
vigorous stanzas, I should. without scruple,
have purposely enfeebled them. so as not to in-
terfere with the climacteric effect.

And here I may as well say a few words of
the verification. My first object (as usual)
was originality. The extent to which this has
been neglected, in versification. is one of the
most unaccountable things in the world. Ad-
mitting that there is little possibility of variety
in mere *rhythm*, it is still clear that the possible varieties of meter and stanza are absolutely infinite—and yet, *for centuries, no man.
in verse, has ever done, or ever seemed to think
of doing, an original thing*. The fact is. originality (unless in minds of very unusual force)
is by no means a matter, as some suppose, of
impulse or intuition. In general, to be found,
it must be elaborately sought, and although a
positive merit of the highest class. demands in

its attainment less of invention than negation.

Of course, I pretend to no originality in either the rhythm or meter of the "Raven." The former is trochaic—the latter is octameter acatalectic, alternating with heptameter catalectic repeated in the *refrain* of the fifth verse. and terminating with tetrameter catalectic. Less pedantically—the feet employed throughout (trochees) consist of a long syllable followed by a short: the first line of the stanza consists of eight of these feet—the second of seven and a half (in effect two-thirds)—the third of eight—the fourth of seven and a half —the fifth the same—the sixth three and a half. Now, each of these lines, taken individually. has been employed before, and what originality the "Raven" has, is in their *combination into stanza;* nothing even remotely approaching this combination has ever been attempted. The effect of this originality of combination is aided by other unusual, and some altogether novel effects. arising from an extension of the application of the principles of rhyme and alliteration.

The next point to be considered was the mode of bringing together the lover and the Raven—and the first branch of this consideration was the *locale.* For this the most natural suggestion might seem to be a forest, or the fields—but it has always appeared to me that a close *circumscription of space* is absolutely necessary to the effect of insulated incident:—it has the force of a frame to a picture. It has an indisputable moral power in keeping concentrated the attention, and, of course, must not be confounded with mere unity of place.

I determined, then, to place the lover in his chamber—in a chamber rendered sacred to him by memories of her who had frequented it. The room is represented as richly furnished— this in mere pursuance of the ideas I have already explained on the subject of Beauty, as the sole true poetical thesis.

The *locale* being thus determined, I had now to introduce the bird—and the thought of introducing him through the window, was inevitable. The idea of making the lover suppose, in the first instance, that the flapping of the wings of the bird against the shutter, is a "tapping" at the door, originated in a wish to increase, by prolonging, the reader's curiosity, and in a desire to admit the incidental effect arising from the lover's throwing open the door, finding all dark, and thence adopting the half-fancy that it was the spirit of his mistress that knocked.

I made the night tempestuous, first, to account for the Raven's seeking admission, and secondly, for the effect of contrast with the (physical) serenity within the chamber.

I made the bird alight on the bust of Pallas, also for the effect of contrast between the marble and the plumage—it being understood that the bust was absolutely *suggested* by the bird—the bust of *Pallas* being chosen, first, as most in keeping with the scholarship of the lover, and, secondly, for the sonorousness of the word, Pallas, itself.

About the middle of the poem, also, I have availed myself of the force of contrast, with a view of deepening the ultimate impression. For example, an air of the fantastic—approaching as nearly to the ludicrous as was admissible—is given to the Raven's entrance. He comes in "with many a flirt and flutter."

"Not the *least obeisance made he*—not a moment
    stopped or stayed he,
 But with mien of lord or lady, perched above my
    chamber door."

In the two stanzas which follow, the design is more obviously carried out:—

"Then this ebony bird beguiling my sad fancy into
   smiling
By the *grave and stern decorum of the counten*ance
   it wore,
'Though thy *crest be shorn and shaven* thou,' I said,
   art sure no craven,
Ghastly grim and ancient Raven wandering from the
   nightly shore—
Tell me what thy lordly name is on the Night's
   Plutonian shore !'
            Quoth the Raven 'Nevermore.'

"Much I marveled *this ungainly fowl* to hear discourse so plainly,
Though its answer little meaning—little relevancy
   bore;
For we cannot help agreeing that no living human
   being
*Ever yet was blessed with seeing bird above his
   chamber door*—
*Bird or beast upon the sculptured bust above his
   chamber door,*
         With such name as 'Nevermore.' "

The effect of the *dénouement* being thus pro-
vided for, I immediately drop the fantastic for
a tone of the most profound seriousness:—this
tone commencing in the stanza directly follow-
ing the one last quoted, with the line,

"But the Raven, sitting lonely on that placid bust,
   spoke only," etc.

From this epoch the lover no longer jests—
no longer sees anything even of the fantastic
in the Raven's demeanor. He speaks of him

as a "grim, ungainly, ghastly, gaunt, and ominous bird of yore," and feels the "fiery eyes" burning into his "bosom's core." This revolution of thought, or fancy, on the lover's part, is intended to induce a similar one on the part of the reader—to bring the mind into a proper frame for the *dénouement*—which is now brought about as rapidly and as *directly* as possible.

With the *dénouement* proper—with the Raven's reply, "Nevermore," to the lover's final demand if he shall meet his mistress in another world—the poem, in its obvious phase, that of a simple narrative, may be said to have its completion. So far, everything is within the limits of the accountable—of the real. A raven, having learned by rote the single word "Nevermore," and having escaped from the custody of its owner, is driven at midnight, through the violence of a storm, to seek admission at a window from which a light still gleams—the chamber-window of a student, occupied half in poring over a volume, half in dreaming of a beloved mistress deceased. The casement being thrown open at the fluttering of the bird's wings, the bird itself perches on the most convenient seat out of the immediate reach of the student, who, amused by the inci-

dent and the oddity of the visitor's demeanor,
demands of it, in jest and without looking for
a reply, its name. The raven addressed, an-
swers with its customary word, "Nevermore"
—a word which finds immediate echo in the
melancholy heart of the student, who, giving
utterance aloud to certain thoughts suggested
by the occasion, is again startled by the fowl's
repetition of "Nevermore." The student now
guesses the state of the case, but is impelled,
as I have before explained, by the human thirst
for self-torture, and in part by superstition, to
propound such queries to the bird as will bring
him, the lover, the most of the luxury of sorrow, through the anticipated answer "Nevermore." With the indulgence, to the utmost
extreme, of this self-torture, the narration, in
what I have termed its first or obvious phase,
has a natural termination, and so far there
has been no overstepping of the limits of the
real.

But in subjects so handled, however skill-
fully, or with however vivid an array of incident, there is always a certain hardness or
nakedness, which repels the artistical eye. Two
things are invariably required—first, some
amount of complexity, or more properly, adap-
tation; and, secondly, some amount of sugges-

tiveness—some undercurrent, however indefi-
nite, of meaning. It is this latter, in especial,
which imparts to a work of art so much of that
richness (to borrow from colloquy a forcible
term) which we are too fond of confounding
with *the ideal*. It is the *excess* of the suggested meaning—it is the rendering this the
upper instead of the under current of the
theme—which turns into prose (and that of
the very flattest kind) the so-called poetry of
the so-called transcendentalists.

Holding these opinions, I added the two concluding stanzas of the poem—their suggestive-
ness being thus made to pervade all the narrative which has preceded them. The undercurrent of meaning is rendered first apparent in
the lines—

" 'Take thy beak from out *my heart,* and take thy
        form from off my door!'
            Quoth the Raven 'Nevermore!' "

It will be observed that the words, "from
out my heart," involve the first metaphorical
expression in the poem. They, with the answer, "Nevermore," dispose the mind to seek
a moral in all that has been previously nar-
rated. The reader begins now to regard the
Raven as emblematical—but it is not until the

very last line of the very last stanza, that the intention of making him emblematical of Mournful and Never-ending Rememberance is permitted distinctly to be seen:

"And the Raven, never flitting, still is sitting,
    still is sitting,
On the pallid bust of Pallas just above my
    chamber door;
And his eyes have all the seeming of a demon's
    that is dreaming,
And the lamplight o'er him streaming throws
    his shadow on the floor;
And my soul from out that shadow that lies
    floating on the floor
        Shall be lifted—nevermore."

THE RAVEN.

Once upon a midnight dreary, while I pondered,
    weak and weary,
Over many a quaint and curious volume of for-
    gotten lore,
While I nodded, nearly napping, suddenly there
    came a tapping,
As of some one gently rapping, rapping at my
    chamber-door.
"Tis some visitor," I muttered, "tapping at my
    chamber-door—
Only this, and nothing more."

Ah, distinctly I remember it was in the bleak
    December,
And each separate dying ember wrought its ghost
    upon the floor.
Eagerly I wished the morrow;—vainly I had tried
    to borrow
From my books surcease of sorrow—sorrow for
    the lost Lenore—
For the rare and radiant maiden whom the Angels
    name Lenore,
Nameless here forevermore.

And the silken sad uncertain rustling of each
    purple curtain
Thrilled me,—filled me with fantastic terrors
    never felt before;
So that now, to still the beating of my heart, I
    stood repeating.

"Tis some visitor entreating entrance at my
    chamber-door;
This it is and nothing more."
Presently my soul grew stronger; hesitating then
    no longer,
"Sir," said I, "or Madam, truly your forgiveness
    I implore;
But the fact is I was napping, and so gently you
    came rapping,

And so faintly you came tapping, tapping at my
    chamber-door,
That I scarce was sure I heard you."—
    Here I opened wide the door;—
Darkness there and nothing more.
Deep into that darkness peering, long I stood
    there wondering, fearing,
Doubting, dreaming dreams no mortal ever dared
    to dream before;

But the silence was unbroken, and the stillness
    gave no token,
And the only word spoken was the whispered
    word "Lenore"—
Merely this and nothing more.
Back into the chamber turning, all my soul within
    me burning,
Soon again I heard a tapping, somewhat louder
    than before.
"Surely," said I. "surely that is something at
    my window-lattice;
Let me see, then, what thereat is, and this
    mystery explore,
Let my heart be still a moment, and this
    mystery explore;
'Tis the wind, and nothing more."

Open here I flung the shutter when, with many
    a flirt and flutter.

In there stepp'd a stately Raven of the saintly
    days of yore.
Not the least obeisance made he; not an instant
    stopped or stayed he;
But with mien of lord or lady, perched above my
    chamber-door,—
Perched upon a bust of Pallas, just above my
    chamber-door,—
Perched, and sat, and nothing more.

Then this ebony bird beguiling my sad fancy
    into smiling,
By the grave and stern decorum of the coun-
    tenance it wore,
"Though thy crest be shorn and shaven, thou,"
    I said, "art sure no craven,
Ghastly, grim, and ancient Raven, wandering
    from the Nightly shore,—
Tell me what thy lordly name is on the Night's
    Plutonian shore."
Quoth the Raven, "Nevermore."

Much I marvelled this ungainly fowl to hear dis-
    course so plainly,
Though its answer little meaning—little relevancy
    bore;
For we cannot help agreeing that no living hu-
    man being
Ever yet was blest with seeing bird above his
    chamber-door—
Bird or beast upon the sculptured bust above
    his chamber-door,
With such name as "Nevermore."

But the Raven, sitting lonely on the placid bust,
    spoke only
That one word, as if his soul in that one word
    he did outpour.

Nothing further then he uttered; not a feather
then he fluttered—
Till I scarcely muttered, "Other friends have
flown before—
On the morrow he will leave me, as my Hopes
have flown before."
Then the bird said, "Nevermore."

Startled at the stillness broken by reply so aptly
spoken,
"Doubtless," said I, "what it utters is its only
stock and store,
Caught from some unhappy master whom unmer-
ciful Disaster
Followed fast and followed faster till his song
one burden bore—
Till the dirges of his Hope that melancholy burden bore—
Of 'Never'—'Nevermore.' "

But the Raven still beguiling all my sad soul
into smiling,
Straight I wheel'd a cushion'd seat in front of
bird, and bust, and door;
Then, upon the velvet sinking, I betook myself
to linking
Fancy unto fancy, thinking what this ominous
bird of yore—
What this grim, ungainly, ghastly, gaunt, and
ominous bird of yore
Meant in croaking "Nevermore."

This I sat engaged in guessing, but no syllable
expressing
To the fowl whose fiery eyes now burned into my
bosom's core;
This and more I sat divining, with my head at
ease reclining

On the cushion's velvet lining that the lamplight
    gloating o'er—
She shall press, ah, nevermore.

Then, methought the air grew denser, perfumed
    from an unseen censer
Swung by Seraphim whose footfalls
    tinkled on the tufted floor.
"Wretch." I cried, "thy God hath lent thee—by
    these angels he hath sent thee
Respite—respite and nepenthe from thy mem-
    ories of Lenore.
Quaff, oh quaff this kind nepenthe, and forget
    this lost Lenore."
Quoth the Raven, "Nevermore."

"Prophet!" said I, "thing of evil, prophet still,
    if bird or devil—
Whether Tempter sent, or whether tempest
    tossed here ashore,
Desolate, yet all undaunted, on this desert land
    enchanted—
On this home by Horror haunted—tell me truly,
    I implore—
Is there—is there balm in Gilead?—tell me, tell
    me, I implore!"
Quoth the Raven, "Nevermore."

"Prophet!" said I, "thing of evil,—prophet still,
    if bird or devil!
By that Heaven that bends above us—by that
    God we both adore—
Tell this soul with sorrow laden, if within the
    distant Aidenn,
It shall clasp a sainted maiden whom the angels
    name Lenore—
Quoth the Raven, "Nevermore."

"Be that word our sign of parting, bird or friend!"
    I shrieked, upstarting—
"Get thee back into the tempest and the Night's
    Plutonian shore!
Leave no black plume as a token of that lie thy
    soul hath spoken!
Leave my loneliness unbroken! quit the bust
    above my door!
Take thy beak from out my heart, and take thy
    form from off my door!"
Quoth the Raven, "Nevermore."

And the Raven, never flitting, still is sitting, still
    is sitting
On the pallid bust of Pallas just above my cham-
    ber door;
And his eyes have all the seeming of a demon's
    that is dreaming,
And the lamplight o'er him streaming throws his
    shadow on the floor;
And my soul from out that shadow that lies float-
    ing on the floor,
Shall be lifted—nevermore!

POEMS WRITTEN IN YOUTH.

Private reasons—some of which have reference to the sin of plagiarism, and others to the date of Tennyson's first poems—have induced me, after some hesitation, to republish these, the crude compositions of my earliest boyhood. They are printed verbatim—without alteration from the original edition*—the date of which is too remote to be judiciously acknowledged.

E. A. P.

*This statement is incorrect.—Ed.

SONNET: TO SCIENCE

Science! true daughter of Old Time thou art!
  Who alterest all things with thy peering eyes.
Why preyest thou thus upon the poet's heart,
  Vulture, whose wings are dull realities?
How should he love thee? or how deem thee wise,
  Who wouldst not leave him in his wandering
To seek for treasure in the jewelled skies,
  Albeit he soared with an undaunted wing?
Hast thou not dragged Diana from her car?
  And driven the Hamadryad from the wood
To seek a shelter in some happier star?
  Hast thou not torn the Naiad from her floor,
The Elfin from the green grass, and from me
  The summer dream beneath the tamarind tree?

AL AARAAF.*

Part I.

Oh! nothing earthly save the ray
(Thrown back from flowers) of Beauty's eye
As in those gardens where the day
Springs from the gems of Circassy—
Oh! nothing earthly save the thrill
Of melody in woodland rill—
Or (music of the passion-hearted)
Joy's voice so peacefully departed

---

*A star was discovered by Tycho Brahe which appeared
suddenly in the heavens—attained, in a few days, a bril-
liancy surpassing that of Jupiter—then as suddenly disappeared, and has never been seen since.

That like the murmur in the shell,
Its echo dwelleth and will dwell—
Oh! nothing of the dross of ours—
Yet all the beauty—all the flowers
That list our Love, and deck our bowers—
Adorn yon world afar, afar—
The wandering star.

'Twas a sweet time for Nesace—for there
Her world lay lolling on the golden air,
Near four bright suns—a temporary rest—
An oasis in the desert of the blest.
Away—away—'mid seas of rays that roll
Empyrean splendor o'er th' unchained soul—
The soul that scarce (the billows are so dense)
Can struggle to its destined eminence—
To distant spheres, from time to time, she rode
And late to ours, the favored one of God—
But, now, the ruler of an anchor'd realm,
She throws aside the sceptre—leaves the helm,
And, amid incense and high spiritual hymns,
Laves in quadruple light her angel limbs.

Now happiest, loveliest in yon lovely Earth,
Whence sprang the "Idea of Beauty" into birth
(Falling in wreaths thro' many a startled star,
Like woman's hair 'mid pearls, until, afar,
It lit on hills Achaian. and there dwelt)
She looked into Infinity—and knelt.
Rich clouds, for canopies, about her curled—
Fit emblems of the model of her world—
Seen but in beauty—not impeding sight
Of other beauty glittering thro' the light—
A wreath that twined each starry form around
And all the opal'd air in color bound.

All hurriedly she knelt upon a bed
Of flowers; of lilies such as rear'd the head

On the fair Capo Deucato,* and sprang
Upon the flying footsteps of—deep pride—
Of her who loved a mortal—and so died.*
The Sephalica, budding with young bees,
Uprear'd its purple stem around her knees;
And gemmy flower, of Trebizond misnam'd†
Inmate of highest stars, where erst it sham'd
All other loveliness; its honied dew
(The fabled nectar that the heathen knew)
Deliriously sweet, was dropp'd from Heaven,
And fell on gardens of the unforgiven
In Trebizond—and on a sunny flower
So like its own above, that, to this hour,
It still remaineth, torturing the bee
With madness, and unwonted reverie;
In Heaven, and all its environs, the leaf
And blossom of the fairy plant, in grief
Disconsolate lingers—grief that hangs her head,
Repenting follies that full long have fled,
Heaving her white breast to the balmly air,
Like guilty beauty, chasten'd, and more fair;
Nyctanthes too, as sacred as the light
She fears to perfume, perfuming the night;
And Clytia pondering between many a sun,‡

---

*On Santa Maura—olim Deucadia.

*Sappho.

†This flower is much noticed by Lewenhoeck and Tournefort. The bee, feeding upon its blossom, becomes intoxicated.

‡Clytia—The Chrysanthemum Peruvianum, or, to employ a better-known term, the turnsol—which turns continually towards the sun, covers itself, like Peru, the country from which it comes, with dewy clouds which cool and refresh its flowers during the most violent heat of the day.—B. de St. Pierre.

While pettish tears adown her petals run;
And that aspiring flower that sprang on Earth*—
And died, ere scarce exalted into birth,
Bursting its odorous heart in spirit to wing
Its way to Heaven, from garden of a king;
And Valisnerian lotus thither flown†
From struggling with the waters of the Rhone:
And thy most lovely purple perfume, Zante!‡
Isola d'oro!—Fior di Levante!
And the Nelumbo bud that floats forever§
With Indian Cupid down the holy river—
Fair flowers, and fairy! to whose care is given
To bear the Goddess' song, in odors, up to
      Heaven:‖

"Spirit! that dwellest where,
  In the deep sky,
The terrible and fair,
  In beauty vie!
Beyond the line of blue—
  The boundary of the star
Which turneth at the view
  Of thy barrier and thy bar—
Of the barrier overgone
  By the comets who were cast
From their pride, and from their throne,
  To be drudges till the last—
To be carriers of fire
  (The red fire of their heart)

---

*There is cultivated in the king's garden at Paris a species of serpentine aloes without prickles, whose large and beautiful flower exhales a strong odor of the vanilla during the time of its expansion, which is very short. It does not blow till towards the month of July; you then perceive it gradually open its petals—expand them —fade—and die.—St. Pierre.

†There is found, in the Rhone, a beautiful lily of the Valisnerian kind. Its stem will stretch to the length of

With speed that may not tire,
  And with pain that shall not part—
Who livest—that we know—
  In Eternity—we feel—
But the shadow of whose brow
  What spirit shall reveal?
Tho' the beings whom thy Nesace,
  Thy messenger hath known
Have dream'd for thy Infinity
  A model of their own—
Thy will is done, O God!
The star hath ridden high
Thro' many a tempest, but she rode
  Beneath thy burning eye;
And here, in thought, to thee—
  In thought that can alone
Ascend thy empire and so be
  A partner of thy throne—
By winged Fantasy
  My embassy is given,
Till secrecy shall knowledge be
  In the environs of Heaven."
  She ceased—and buried then her burning cheek,
Abashed, amid the lilies there, to seek
A shelter from the fervor of His eye;
For the stars trembled at the Deity.
She stirred not—breathed not—for a voice was
    there
How solemnly pervading the calm air!

---

three or four feet—thus preserving its head above water
in the swellings of the river.
  ‡The Hyacinth.
  §It is a fiction of the Indians that Cupid was first seen
floating in one of these down the river Ganges, and that
he still loves the cradle of his childhood.
  ‖And golden vials full of odors, which are the prayers
of the saints.—Rev. of St. John.

A sound of silence on the startled ear
Which dreamy poets name "the music of the
    sphere."
Ours is a world of words: Quiet we call
"Silence"—which is the merest word of all.
All nature speaks, and ev'n ideal things
Flap shadowy sounds from visionary wings—
But ah! not so when, thus, in realms on high
The eternal voice of God is passing by,
And the red wings are withering in the sky!

  "What tho' in worlds which sightless cycles
      run,*
Link'd to a little system, and one sun—
Where all my love is folly and the crowd
Still think my terrors but the thunder-cloud,
The storm, the earthquake, and the ocean-wrath—
(Ah! will they cross me in my angrier path?)
What tho' in worlds which own a single sun
The sands of time grow dimmer as they run,
Yet thine is my resplendency, so given
To bear my secrets thro' the upper Heaven.
Leave tenantless thy crystal home, and fly,
With all thy train, athwart the moony sky—
Apart—like fireflies in Sicilian night,*
And wing to other worlds another light!
Divulge the secrets of thy embassy
To the proud orbs that twinkle—and so be
To ev'ry heart a barrier and a ban
Lest the stars totter in the guilt of man!"

  Up rose the maiden in the yellow night,
The single-mooned eve!—on Earth we plight

---

*Sightless—too small to be seen.—Legge.

*I have often noticed a peculiar movement of the
fireflies—they will collect in a body and fly off, from a

Our faith to one love—and one moon adore—
The birthplace of young Beauty had no more.
As sprang that yellow star from downy hours,
Up rose the maiden from her shrine of flowers,
And bent o'er sheeny mountain and dim plain
Her way—but left not yet her Therasaean reign.†

Part II.

High on a mountain of enamelled head—
Such as the drowsy shepherd on his bed
Of giant pasturage lying at his ease,
Raising his heavy eyelid, starts and sees
With many a muttered "hope to be forgiven"
What time the moon is quadrated in Heaven—
Of rosy head, that towering far away
Into the sunlit ether, caught the ray
Of sunken suns at eve—at noon of night,
While the moon danced with the fair stranger
        light—
Upreared upon such height arose a pile
Of gorgeous columns on th' unburthen'd air,
Flashing from Parian marble that twin smile
Far down upon the wave that sparkled there,
And nursled the young mountain in its lair.
Of molten stars their pavement, such as fall*
Thro' the ebon air, besilvering the pall
Of their own dissolution, while they die—
Adorning then the dwellings of the sky.
A dome, by linked light from Heaven let down
Sat gently on these columns as a crown—

---

common center, into innumerable radii.

†Therasaea, or Therasea, the island mentioned by Se-
neca, which, in a moment, arose from the sea to the eyes
of astonished mariners.

*Some star which, from the ruin'd roof
  Of shak'd Olympus, by mischance, did fall.—Milton.

A window of one circular diamond, there,
Lock'd out above into the purple air,
And rays from God shot down that meteor chain
And hallow'd all the beauty twice again,
Save when, between th' Empyrean and that ring,
Some eager spit flapp'd his dusky wing.
But on the pillars Seraph eyes have seen
The dimness of this world: that grayish green
That nature loves the best for Geauty's grave
Lurked in each cornice, round each architrave—
And every sculptured cherub thereabout
That from his marble dwelling peered out,
Seemed earthly in the shadow of his niche—
Achaian statues in a world so rich?
Friezes from Tadmor and Persepolis
From Baalbec, and the stilly, clear abyss
Of beautiful Gomorrha! O, the wave*
Is now upon thee—but too late to save!

Sound loves to revel in a summer night:
Witness the murmur of the gray twilight
That stole upon the ear, in Eyraco,†

---

*"O, the wave"—Ulga Deguisi is the Turkish appellation; but, on its own shores, it is called Bahar Loth, or Almotanah.   There were undoubtedly more than two cities engulphed in the "Dead Sea." In the Valley of Siddim were five—Admah, Zeboim, Zoar, Sodom and Gommorrha. Stephen of Byzantium mentions eight, and Strabo thirteen (engulphed)—but the last is out of all reason.
It is said (Tacitus, Strabo, Josephus, Daniel of St. Saba, Nau, Maundrell, Troilo, D'Arvieux) that after an excessive drought, the vestiges of columns, walls, etc., are seen above the surface. At any season, such remains may be discovered by looking down into the transparent lake, and at such distance as would argue the existence of many settlements in the space now usurped by the "Asphalites."
†Eyraco.—Chaldea.

Of many a wild star-gazer long ago—
That stealeth ever on the ear of him
Who, musing, gazeth on the distance dim,
And sees the darkness coming as a cloud—
Is not its form—its voice—most palpable and
    loud?*

But what is this!—It cometh—and it brings
A music with it— tis the rush of wings—
A pause—and then a sweeping, falling strain,
And Nesace is in her halls again.
From the wild energy of wanton haste
  Her cheeks were flushing, and her lips apart;
And zone that clung around her gentle waist
  Had burst beneath the heaving of her heart.
Within the center of that hall to breathe
She paus'd and panted, Zanthe! all beneath
The fairy light that kiss'd her golden hair,
And long'd to rest, yet could but sparkle there!

Young flowers were whispering in melody†
To happy flowers that night—and tree to tree:
Fountains were gushing music as they fell
In many a star-lit grove, or moon-lit-dell;
Yet silence came upon material things—
Fair flowers, bright waterfalls and angel wings—
And sound alone that from the spirit sprang
Bore burthen to the charm the maiden sang:

  "'Neath the blue-bell or streamer—
  Or tufted wild spray
  That keeps, from the dreamer,

---

*I have often thought I could distinctly hear the sound of the darkness as it stole over the horizon.

†"Fairies use flowers for their charactery."—Merry Wives of Windsor.

The moonbean away*—
Bright beings! that ponder,
  With half closing eyes,
On the stars which your wonder
  Hath drawn from the skies,
Till they glance thro' the shade, and
  Come down to your brow
Like—eyes of the maiden
  Who calls on you now—
Arise! from your dreaming
  In violet bowers,
To duty beseeming
  These star-litten hours—
And shake from your tresses
  Encumber'd with dew
The breath of those kisses
  That cumber them too
(O! how, without you, Love!
  Could angels be blest?)
Those kisses of true love
  That lull'd ye to rest!
Up!—shake from your wing
  Each hindering thing:
The dew of the night—
  It would weigh down your flight;
And true love caresses—
  O! leave them apart!
They are light on the tresses,
  But lead on the heart.

---

*In Scripture is this passage—"The sun shall not smite thee by day, nor the moon by night." It is perhaps not generally known that the moon, in Egypt, has the effect of producing blindness to those who sleep with the face exposed to its rays, to which circumstance the passage evidently alludes.

Ligeia! Ligeia!
  My beautiful one!
Whose harshest idea
  Will to melody run,
O! is it thy will
  On the breezes to toss?
Or, capriciously still,
  Like the lone Albatross,*
Incumbent on night
  (As she on the air)
To keep watch with delight
On the harmony there?

Ligeia! wherever
  Thy image may be,
No magic shall sever
  Thy music from thee
Thou hast bound many eyes
  In a dreamy sleep—
But the strains still arise
  Which thy vigilance keep—
The sound of the rain,
  Which leaps down to the flower
And dances again
  In the rhythm of the shower—
The murmur that springs*
  From the growing of grass—
Are the music of things—
  But are modell'd, alas!—
Away, then, my dearest,
  O! hie thee away

---

*The Albatross is said to sleep on the wing.

*I met this idea in an old English tale, which I am now unable to obtain, and quote from memory.—"The verie essence, and, as it were, springeheade and origine of all musicke is the verie pleasaunte sounde which the trees of the forest do make when they growe."

To springs that lie clearest
  Beneath the moon-ray—
To lone lake that smiles,
  In its dream of deep rest,
At the many star-isles
  That enjewel its breast—
Where wild flowers, creeping,
  Have mingled their shade,
On its margin is sleeping
  Full many a maid—
Some have left the cool glade, and
  Have slept with the bee—
Arouse them, my maiden,
  On moorland and lea—
Go! breathe on their slumber,
  All softly in ear,
The musical number
  They slumber'd to hear—
For what can awaken
  An angel so soon
Whose sleep hath been taken
  Beneath the cold moon,
As the spell which no slumber
  Of witchery may test,
The rhythmical number
  Which lulled him to rest?"

Spirits in wing, and angels to the view,
A thousand seraphs burst th' Empyrean thro',

---

*The wild bee will not sleep in the shade if there be
moonlight.

The rhyme in this verse, as in one about sixty lines
before, has an appearance of affectation. It is, however,
imitated from Sir Walter Scott, or rather from Claud
Halcro—in whose mouth I admired its effect—

  "Oh! were there an island
  Tho' ever so wild,
Where woman might smile, and
  No man be beguiled," etc.

Young dreams still hovering on their drowsy
    flight—
Seraphs in all but "Knowledge," the keen light
That fell, refracted, thro' thy bounds, afar,
O Death! from eye of God upon that star:
Sweet was that error—sweeter still that death—
Sweet was that error—ev'n with us the breath
Of Science dims the mirror of our joy—
To them 'twere the Simoon, and would destroy—
For what (to them) availeth it to know
That Truth is Falsehood—or that Bliss is Woe?
Sweet was their death—with them to die was rife
With the last ecstasy of satiate life—
Beyond that death no immortality—
But sleep that pondereth and is not "to be"—
And there—oh! may my weary spirit dwell—
Apart from Heaven's Eternity—and yet how far
    from Hell!*
What guilty spirit, in what shrubbery dim,
Heard not the stirring summons of that hymn?
But two: they fell: for Heaven no grace imparts
To those who hear not for their beating hearts.
A maiden angel and her seraph-lover—
O! where (and ye may seek the wide skies over)
Was Love, the blind, near sober Duty known?
Unguided Love hath fallen—'mid "tears of per-
    fect moan."*

He was a goodly spirit—he who fell:
A wanderer by the moss-y-mantled well—

---

*With the Arabians there is a medium between Heaven
and Hell, where men suffer no punishment, but yet do
not attain that tranquil and even happiness which they
suppose to be characteristic of heavenly enjoyment.

Sorrow is not excluded from "Al Aaraaf," but it is that
sorrow which the living love to cherish for the dead, and
which in some minds resembles the delirium of opium

A gazer on the lights that shine above—
A dreamer in the moonbeam by his love:
What wonder? for each star is eye-like there
And looks so sweetly down on Beauty's hair—
And they, and every mossy spring were holy
To his love-haunted heart and melancholy.
The night had found (to him a night of wo)
Upon a mountain crag, young Angelo
Beetling its bends athwart the solemn sky,
And scowls on starry worlds that down beneath
    it lie.
Here sat he with his love—his dark eye bent
With eagle gaze along the firmament;
Now turned it upon her—but ever then
It trembled to the orb of Earth again

"Ianthe, dearest, see! how dim that ray!
How lovely 'tis to look so far away!
She seem'd not thus upon that autumn eve
I left her gorgeous halls—nor mourn'd to leave,
That eve—that eve—I should remember well—
The sun-ray dropp'd, in Lemnos, with a spell
On th' Arabesque carving of a gilded hall
Wherein I sate, and on the draperied wall—
And on my eye-lids—O, the heavy light!
How drowsily it weighed them into night!
On flowers, before, and mist, and love they ran
With Persion Saadi in his Gullistan:
But O, that light!—I slumbered—Death, the while
Stole o'er my senses in that lovely isle

The passionate excitement of Love, and the buoyancy of
spirit attendant upon intoxication, are its less holy plea-
sures—the price of which, to those souls who make choice
of "Al Aaraaf" as their residence after life, is final
death and annihilation.
    *"There be tears of perfect moan
    Wept for thee in Helicon."—Milton.

So softly that no single silken hair
Awoke that sleep—or knew that he was there.

"The last spot of Earth's orb I trod upon
Was a proud temple called the Parthenon;*
More beauty clung around her columned wall
Than even thy glowing bosom beats withal,
And when old Time my wing did disenthral
Thence sprang I—as the eagle from his tower,
And years I left behind me in an hour.
What time upon her airy bounds I hung
One half the garden of her globe was flung
Unrolling as a chart unto my view—
Tenantless cities of the desert too!
Ianthe, beauty crowded on me then,
And half I wished to be again of of men."

"My Angelo! and why of them to be?
A brighter dwelling place is here for thee—
And greener fields than in yon world above,
And woman's loveliness—and passionate love."

"But list, Ianthe, when the air so soft
Failed, as my pennon'd-sipirit leapt aloft,†
Perhaps my brain grew dizzy—but the world
I left so late was into chaos hurl'd,
Sprang from her station, on the winds apart,
And rolled a flame, the fiery Heavens athwart.
Methought, my sweet one, then I ceased to soar,
And fell—not swiftly as I rose before,
But with a downward, tremulous motion thro'
Light, brazen rays, this golden star unto!

---

*It was entire in 1687—the most elevated spot in Athens.
*"Shadowing more beauty in their airy brows
  Than have the white breasts of the queen of love."
†Pennon, for pinion.—Milton.

—Marlowe.

Nor long the measure of my falling hours,
For nearest to all stars was thine to ours—
Dread star! that came, amid a night of mirth,
A red Daedalion on the timid Earth."

"We came—and to thy Earth—but not to us
Be given our lady's bidding to discuss:
We came, my love; around, above, below,
Gay fire-fly of the night we come and go,
Nor ask a reason save the angel-nod
She grants to us as granted by her God—
But, Angelo, than thine grey Time unfurled
Never his fairy wing o'er fairer world!
Dim was its little disk, and angel eyes
Alone could see the phantom in the skies,
When first Al Aaraaf knew her course to be
Headlong thitherward o'er the starry sea—
But when its glory swelled upon the sky,
As glowing Beauty's bust beneath man's eye,
We paused before the heritage of men,
And thy star trembled—as doth Beauty then!"

Thus in discourse, the lovers whiled away
The night that waned and waned and brought no
        day.
They fell: for Heaven to them no hope imparts
Who hear not for the beating of their hearts.

TAMERLANE.

Kind solace in a dying hour!
    Such, father, is not (now) my theme—
I will not madly deem that power
        Of Earth may shrive me of the sin
        Unearthly pride hath revell'd in—
    I have no time to dote or dream:
You call it hope—that fire of fire!

It is but agony of desire
If I can hope—O God! I can—
  Its fount is holier—more divine—
I would not call thee fool, old man,
  But such is not a gift of thine.

Know thou the secret of a spirit
  Bowed from its wild pride into shame,
O yearning heart! I did inherit
  Thy withering portion with the fame,
The searing glory which hath shone
Amid the Jewels of my throne,
Halo of Hell! and with a pain
Not Hell shall make me fear again—
O craving heart, for the lost flowers
And sunshine of my summer hours!
The undying voice of that death time,
With its interminable chime,
Rings, in the spirit of a spell,
Upon thy emptiness—a knell.

I have not always been as now:
The fevered diadem on my brow
  I claimed and won usurpingly—
Hath not the same fierce heirdom given
  Rome to the Caesar—this to me?
    The heritage of a kingly mind,
And a proud spirit which hath striven
    Triumphantly with human kind.

On mountain soil I first drew life:
  The mists of the Taglay have shed
  Nightly their dews upon my head,
And, I believe, the winged strife
  And tumult of the headlong air
  Have nestled in my very hair.

So late from Heaven—that dew—it fell
  ('Mid dreams of an unholy night)

Upon me with the touch of Hell,
　While the red flashing of the light
From clouds that hung, like banners, o'er,
　Appeared to my half-closing eye
　The pageantry of monarchy,
And the deep trumpet thunder's roar
　Came hurriedly upon me, telling
　　Of human battle, where my voice,
　My own voice, silly child!—was swelling
　　(O! how my spirit would rejoice,
And leap within me at the cry)
The battle-cry of Victory!

The rain came down upon my head
　Unshelter'd—and the heavy wind
　Rendered me mad and deaf and blind.
It was but man, I thought, who shed
　Laurels upon me: and the rush—
The torrent of the chilly air
　Gurgled within my ear the crush
Of empires—with the captive's prayer—
　The hum of suitors—and the tone
　Of flattery 'round a sovereign's throne.

My passions, from that hapless hour
　Usurped a tyranny which men
Have deemed since I reached to power
　　My innate nature—be it so:
　But, father, there lived one who, then,
Then—in my boyhood—when their fire
　　Burn'd with a still intenser glow
(For passion must, with youth, inspire)
　E'en then who knew this iron heart
　In woman's weakness had a part.

　I have no words—alas!—to tell
　The loveliness of loving well!
　Nor would I now attempt to trace

The more than beauty of a face
Whose lineaments, upon my mind,
Are—shadows on th' unstable wind.
Thus I remember having dwelt
　　Some page of early lore upon,
With loitering eye, till I have felt
The letters—with their meaning—melt
　　To fantasies—with none.

O, she was worthy of all love!
　　Love—as in infancy—was mine—
'Twas such as angel minds above
　　Might envy: her young heart the shrine
On which my every hope and thought
　　Were incense—then a goodly gift,
　　For they were childish and upright—
Pure—as her young example taught:
　　Why did I leave it, and, adrift,
　　　　Trust to the fire within, for light?

We grew in age—and love—together—
　　Roaming the forest, and the wild;
My breast her shield in wintry weather—
　　And, when the friendly sunshine smiled,
And she would mark the opening skies,
I saw no heaven—but in her eyes.

Young Love's first lesson is—the heart;
　　For 'mid that sunshine and those smiles
When, from our little cares apart,
　　And laughing at her girlish wiles,
I'd throw me on her throbbing breast,
　　And pour my spirit out in tears—
There was no need to speak the rest—
　　No need to quiet any fears
Of her—who ask'd no reason why,
But turn'd on me her quiet eye!

Yet more than worthy of the love
My spirit struggled with, and strove,
    When, on the mountain peak alone,
    Ambition lent it a new tone—
I had no being—but in thee:
    The world and all it did contain
In the earth—the air—the sea—
    Its joy—its little lot of pain
That was new pleasure—the ideal,
    Dim vanities of dreams by night—
And dimmer nothings which were real—
    (Shadows—and a more shadowy light!)
Parted upon their misty wings,
    And so, confusedly, became
    Thine image and—a name—a name!
Two separate—yet most intimate things.

I was ambitious—have you known
    The passion, father? You have not:
A cottager, I mark'd a throne
Of half the world as all my own,
    And murmur'd at such lowly lot—
But, 'just like any other dream,
    Upon the vapor of the dew
My own had past, did not the beam
    Of beauty which did while it thro'
The minute—the hour—the day—oppress
My mind with double loveliness.
We walk'd together on the crown
Of a high mountain which looked down
Afar from its proud natural towers
    Of rock and forest,, on the hills—
The dwindled hills! begirt with bowers
    And shouting with a thousand rills.

I spoke to her of power and pride,
    But mystically—in such guise
That she might deem it nought beside
    The moment's converse; in her eyes

read, perhaps too carelessly—
A mingled feeling with my own—
The flush on her bright cheek, to me
  Seem'd to become a queenly throne
Too well that I should let it be
  Light in the wilderness alone.

I wrapp'd myself in grandeur then,
  And donn'd a visionary crown—
  Yet it was not that Fantasy
  Had thrown her mantle over me—
But that, among the rabble—men,
  Lion Ambition is chain'd down—
And crouches to a keeper's hand—
Not so in deserts where the grand—
  The wild—the terrible conspire
  With their own breath to fan his fire.

Look 'round thee now on Samarcand!—
  Is she not queen of Earth? her price
Above all cities? in her hand
  Their destinies? in all beside
Of glory which the world hath known
Stands she not nobly and alone?
Falling—her veriest stepping-stone
Shall form the pedestal of a throne—
  And who her sovereign? Timour—he
  Whom the astonished people saw
  Striding o'er empires haughtily
  A diadem'd outlaw?

O, human love! thou spirit given,
On Earth, of all we hope in Heaven!
Which fall'st into the soul like rain
Upon the Siroc-withered plain,
And, failing in thy power to bless,
But leav'st the heart a wilderness!
Idea! which bindest life around

With music of so strange a sound
And beauty of so wild a birth—
Farewell! for I have won the earth.
When Hope, that eagle that tower'd, could see
  No cliff beyond him in the sky,
His pinions were bent droopingly—
  And homeward turn'd his softened eye.
'Twas sunset: when the sun will part
There comes a sullenness of heart
To him who still would look upon
The glory of all the summer sun.
That soul will hate the ev'ning mist
So often lovely, and will list
To the sound of the coming darkness (known
To those whose spirits hearken) as one
Who, in a dream of night, would fly,
But cannot, from a danger nigh.

What tho' the moon—the white moon
Shed all the splendor of her noon,
Her smile is chilly—and her beam,
In that time of dreariness, will seem
(So like you gather in your breath)
A portrait taken after death.
And boyhood is a summer sun
Whose waning is the dreariest one—
For all we live to know is known
And all we seek to keep hath flown—
Let life, then, as the day flower, fall
With the noon-day beauty—which is all.
I reach'd my home—my home no more—
  For all had flown who made it so.
I passed from out its mossy door,
  And, tho' my thread was soft and low
A voice came from the threshold stone
Of one whom I had earlier known—
  O, I defy thee, Hell, to show
  Beds of fire that burn below,
  An humbler heart—a deeper woe.

Father, I firmly do believe—
  I know—for Death who comes for me
    From regions of the blest afar,
Where there is nothing to deceive,
    Hath left his iron gate ajar,
  And rays of truth you cannot see
  Are flashing thro' Eternity—
I do believe that Eblis hath
A snare in every human path—
Else how, when in the holy grove
I wandered of the idol, Love—
Who daily scents the snowy wings
With incense of burnt-offerings
From the most unpolluted things
Whose pleasant bowers are yet so riven
Above with trellis'd rays from Heaven
No mote may shun—no tiniest fly—
The light'ning of his eagle eye—
How was it that Ambition crept,
  Unseen, amid the revels there,
Till growing bold, he laughed and leapt
  In the tangles of Love's very hair?

A DREAM.

In visions of the dark night
  I have dreamed of joy departed—
But a waking dream of life and light
  Hath left me broken-hearted.

Ah! what is not a dream by day
  To him whose eyes are cast
On things around him with a ray
  Turned back upon the past?

That holy dream—that holy dream,
  While all the world were chiding,
    Hath cheered me as a lovely beam
  A lonely spirit guiding.

What though that light, thro' storm and night
  So trembled from afar—
What could there be more purely bright
  In Truth's day-star?

ROMANCE.

Romance, who loves to nod and sing,
With drowsy head and folded wing,
Among the green leaves as they shake
Far down within some shadowy lake.
To me a painted paroquet
Hath been—a most familiar bird—
Taught me my alphabet to say—
To lisp my very earliest words
While in the wild wood I did lie,
A child—with a most knowing eye.
Of late, eternal Condor years
So shake the very Heaven on high
With tumult as they thunder by,
I have no time for idle cares
Through gazing on the unquiet sky,
And when an hour with calmer wings
Its down upon my spirit flings—
That little time with lyre and rhyme
To while away—forbidden things!
My heart would feel to be a crime
Unless it trembled with the strings.

FAIRYLAND.

Dim vales—and shadowy floods—
And cloudy looking woods,

Whose forms we can't discover
For the tears that drip all over
Huge moons there wax and wane—
Again—again—again—
Every moment of the night—
For ever changing places—
And they put out the star-light
With the breath from their pale faces.
About twelve by the moon-dial
One more filmy than the rest
(A kind which, upon trial,
They have found to be the best)
Comes down—still down—and down
With its center on the crown
Of a mountain's eminence,
While its wide circumference
In easy drapery falls
Over hamlets, over halls,
Wherever they may be—
O'er the strange woods—o'er the sea—
Over spirits on the wing—
Over every drowsy thing—
And buries them up quite
In a labyrinth of light—
And then how deep!—O, deep!
Is the passion of their sleep.
In the morning they arise,
And their moony covering
Is soaring in the skies,
With the tempests as they toss,
Like—almost anything—
Or a yellow Albatross.
They use that moon no more
For the same end as before—
Videlicet a tent—
Which I think extravagant.
Its atomies, however,
Into a shower dissever.

Of which those butterflies
Of Earth, who seek the skies,
And so come down again
(Never-contented things!)
Have brought a specimen
Upon their quivering wings.

TO ———.

The bowers whereat, in dreams, I see
  The wantonest singing birds,
Are lips—and all thy melody
  Of lip-begotten words—

Thine eyes, in Heaven of heart enshrined
  Then desolately fall,
O God! on my funereal mind
  Like starlight on a pall—

Thy heart—thy heart!—I wake and sigh,
  And sleep to dream till day
Of the truth that gold can never buy—
  Of the baubles that it may.

TO THE RIVER ———.

Fair river! in thy bright, clear flow
  Of crystal, wandering water,
Thou art an emblem of the glow
    Of beauty—the unhidden heart—-
    The playful maziness of art
  In old Alberto's daughter;

But when within thy wave she looks—
  Which glistens then, and trembles—
Why, then, the prettiest of books

Her worshipper resembles;
For in his heart, as in thy stream,
  Her image deeply lies—
His heart which trembles at the beam
  Of her soul-searching eyes.

THE LAKE. TO ———.

In spring of youth it was my lot
To haunt of the wide world a spot
The which I could not love the less—
So lovely was the loneliness
Of a wild lake, with black rock bound,
And the tall pines that towered around.
But when the Night had thrown her pall

Upon that spot, as upon all,
And the mystic wind went by
Murmuring in melody—
Then—ah, then, I would awake
To the terror of the lone lake.
Yet that terror was not fright,
But a tremulous delight—
A feeling not the jewelled mine
Could teach or bribe me to define
Nor Love—although the Love were thine.
Death was in that poisonous wave,
And in its gulf a fitting grave
For him who thence could solace bring
To his lone imagining—
Whose solitary soul could make
An Eden of that dim lake.

SONG.

I saw thee on thy bridal day—
  When a burning blush came o'er thee.
Though happiness around thee lay,
  The world all love before thee:

And in thine eye a kindling light
  (Whatever it might be)
Was all on Earth my aching sight
  Of Loveliness could see.

That blush, perhaps, was maiden shame—
  As such it well may pass—
Though its glow hath raised a fiercer flame
  In the breast of him, alas!

Who saw thee on that bridal day,
  When that deep blush would come o'er thee
Though happiness around thee lay,
  The world all love before thee.

Later Poems

A DREAM WITHIN A DREAM.

Take this kiss upon the brow!
And, in parting from you now,
Thus much let me avow—
You are not wrong, who deem
That my days have been a dream;
Yet if hope has flown away
In a night, or in a day,
In a vision, or in none,
Is it therefore the less gone?
All that we see or seem
Is but a dream within a dream.

I stand amid the roar
Of a surf-tormented shore,
And I hold within my hand
Grains of the golden sand—
How few! yet how they creep
Through my fingers to the deep,
While I weep—while I weep!
O God! can I not grasp
Them with a tighter clasp?
O God! can I not save
One from the pitiless wave?
Is all that we see or seem
But a dream within a dream?

TO HELEN.

I saw thee once—once only—years ago:
I must not say how many—but not many.
It was a July midnight; and from out

A full-orbed moon, that, like thine own **soul,
      soaring,**
Sought a precipitate pathway up through **heaven,**
There fell a silvery-silken veil of light,
With quietude, and sultriness, and slumber,
Upon the upturn'd faces of a thousand
Roses that grew in an enchanted garden,
Where no wind dared to stir, unless on tiptoe—
Fell on the upturn'd faces of these roses
That gave out, in return for the love-light,
Their odorous souls in an ecstatic death—
Fell on the upturn'd faces of these roses
That smiled and died in this parterre, **enchanted**
By thee, and by the poetry of thy presence
Clad all in white, upon a violet bank
I saw thee half-reclining; while the moon
Fell on the upturn'd faces of the roses,
And on thine own, upturn'd—alas! in sorrow!
Was it not Fate, that, on this July midnight—
Was it not Fate (whose name is also Sorrow),
That bade me pause before that garden gate,
To breathe the incense of those slumbering roses?
No footstep stirred: the hated world all slept,
Save only thee and me—(O Heaven!—O God!
How my heart beats in coupling those two words!)
Save only thee and me. I paused—I looked—
And in an instant all things disappeared.
(Ah, bear in mind this garden was enchanted!)
The pearly lustre of the moon went out:
The mossy banks and the meandering paths,
The happy flowers and the repining trees,
Were seen no more: the very roses' odors
Died in the arms of the adoring airs.
All—all expired save thee—save less than **thou:**
Save only the divine light in thine eyes—
Save but the soul in thine uplifted eyes.
I saw but them—they were the world to me.
I saw but them—saw only them for hours—
Saw only them until the moon went down.

What wild heart-histories seemed to lie enwrit-
ten
Upon those crystalline, celestial spheres!
How dark a wo! yet how sublime a hope!
How silently serene a seat of pride!
How daring an ambition! yet how deep,
How fathomless a capacity for love!

But now, at length, dear Dian sank from sight,
Into a western couch of thunder-cloud;
And thou, a ghost, amid the entombing trees
Didst glide away. Only thine eyes remained.
They would not go—they never yet have gone.
Lighting my lonely pathway home that night,
They have not left me (as my hopes have) since
They follow me—they lead me through the years.
They are my ministers—yet I their slave.
Their office is to illumine and enkindle—
My duty, to be saved by their bright light,
And purified in their electric fire,
And sanctified in their elysian fire.
They fill my soul with Beauty (which is Hope),
And are far up in Heaven—the stars I kneel to
In the sad, silent watches of my night;
While even in the meridian glare of day
I see them still—two sweetly scintillant
Venuses, unextinguished by the sun!

CPSIA information can be obtained at www.ICGtesting.com
Printed in the USA
BVOW010246271211

279214BV00001B/10/A